GAO

Report to the Committee on Energy and Commerce, House of Representatives

I0455421

April 2013

NATIONAL PREPAREDNESS

Efforts to Address the Medical Needs of Children in a Chemical, Biological, Radiological, or Nuclear Incident

GAO

Accountability ★ Integrity ★ Reliability

GAO-13-438

GAO
Accountability * Integrity * Reliability

Highlights

Highlights of GAO-13-438, a report to the Committee on Energy and Commerce, House of Representatives

NATIONAL PREPAREDNESS

Efforts to Address the Medical Needs of Children in a Chemical, Biological, Radiological, or Nuclear Incident

Why GAO Did This Study

The nation remains vulnerable to terrorist and other threats posed by CBRN agents. Medical countermeasures—drugs, vaccines, and medical devices—can prevent or treat the effects of exposure to CBRN agents, and countermeasures are available in the SNS for some of these agents. Children, who make up 25 percent of the population in the United States, are especially vulnerable because many of the countermeasures in the SNS have only been approved for use in adults. HHS leads the federal efforts to develop and acquire countermeasures.

GAO was asked about efforts to address the needs of children in the event of a CBRN incident. This report examines (1) the percentage of CBRN medical countermeasures in the SNS that are approved for pediatric use; (2) the challenges HHS faces in developing and acquiring CBRN medical countermeasures for the pediatric population, and the steps it is taking to address them; and (3) the ways that HHS has addressed the dispensing of pediatric medical countermeasures in its emergency response plans and guidance, and ways that state and local governments have addressed this issue. To address these objectives, GAO reviewed relevant laws, agency documents, and reports, and interviewed HHS officials, industry representatives, and subject-matter experts. GAO also reviewed a stratified sample of emergency response plans from seven state and seven local governments, based on geographic location and population size, to assess how these governments address pediatric dispensing.

View GAO-13-438. For more information, contact Marcia Crosse at (202) 512-7114 or crossem@gao.gov.

What GAO Found

According to the Department of Health and Human Services (HHS), about 60 percent of the chemical, biological, radiological, and nuclear (CBRN) medical countermeasures in the Strategic National Stockpile (SNS) have been approved for children, but in many instances approval is limited to specific age groups. In addition, about 40 percent of the CBRN countermeasures have not been approved for any pediatric use. Furthermore, some of the countermeasures have not been approved to treat individuals for the specific indications for which they have been stockpiled. For example, ciprofloxacin is stockpiled in the SNS for the treatment of anthrax, plague, and tularemia, but is not approved for these indications. Countermeasures may be used to treat unapproved age groups or indications under an emergency use authorization (EUA) or an Investigational New Drug (IND) application submitted to the Food and Drug Administration (FDA).

HHS faces a variety of economic, regulatory, scientific, and ethical challenges in developing and acquiring pediatric CBRN medical countermeasures. High costs and the high risk of failure associated with testing and research of pharmaceutical products on children, difficulties in meeting regulatory requirements for approving CBRN countermeasures, and scientific and ethical obstacles to safely evaluating countermeasures for children all pose challenges to developing pediatric countermeasures. Despite these challenges, HHS has taken steps to focus agency efforts on the pediatric population, adapt pediatric formulations from existing medical countermeasures, and prepare and review materials for EUAs and INDs in advance of public health emergencies.

HHS addresses dispensing of pediatric medical countermeasures in more than half of its 12 response plans and in its guidance, and seven state and seven local government plans that GAO reviewed included details about pediatric dispensing. Seven of the 12 HHS plans include information about pediatric medical countermeasures; however, HHS officials stated that these plans are intended to provide guidance for emergency response at the federal level, and not at the state or local levels, which is where dispensing would occur. CDC and FDA also provide guidance on pediatric dispensing that state and local governments can use in their planning. For example, CDC developed guidance about receiving, distributing, and dispensing contents from the SNS to help state and local emergency management and public health personnel plan for the use of countermeasures from the SNS. Response plans for all 14 of the state and local governments that GAO reviewed also included details about dispensing to the pediatric population during an emergency. For example, these seven states and seven local governments all adopted some version of a "family member pick-up" policy—sometimes referred to as a "head of household" policy—which would allow adults to pick up medicines for other family members, including children, during an event.

In commenting on a draft of this report, HHS concurred with our findings. HHS emphasized that the needs of the pediatric population have been a priority for HHS and that the department is continuously progressing in this area.

United States Government Accountability Office

Contents

Abbreviations

ASPR	Office of the Assistant Secretary for Preparedness and Response
AVA	anthrax vaccine adsorbed
BARDA	Biomedical Advanced Research and Development Authority
CBRN	chemical, biological, radiological, and nuclear
CDC	Centers for Disease Control and Prevention
CHILD	Children's HHS Interagency Leadership on Disasters
DHS	Department of Homeland Security
EUA	Emergency Use Authorization
FDA	Food and Drug Administration
HHS	Department of Health and Human Services
IND	Investigational New Drug
NIH	National Institutes of Health
PHEMCE	Public Health Emergency Medical Countermeasures Enterprise
POD	point of dispensing
SNS	Strategic National Stockpile

United States Government Accountability Office
Washington, DC 20548

April 30, 2013

The Honorable Fred Upton
Chairman
The Honorable Henry Waxman
Ranking Member
Committee on Energy and Commerce
House of Representatives

The 2001 anthrax attacks and the 2011 earthquake and tsunami in Japan raised concerns that the United States is vulnerable to intentional and unintentional threats from chemical, biological, radiological, and nuclear (CBRN) agents.[1] Rapid diagnosis, treatment, and prevention could mitigate the public health impact of a release of CBRN agents, and there are medical countermeasures available for some of these agents.[2] Members of Congress, federal commissions, and other experts have noted the need for the United States to develop and acquire medical countermeasures to protect the public, and children in particular, from public health emergencies involving CBRN agents. In 2010, the National Commission on Children and Disasters reported that children, who make up nearly 25 percent of the U.S. population, are more susceptible to CBRN threats and require different countermeasures, dosages, and delivery systems than adults.[3]

The Department of Health and Human Services (HHS) is responsible for leading federal efforts to prepare for and respond to public health and medical CBRN incidents, including identifying needed medical countermeasures to diagnose, treat, prevent, or mitigate potential health effects from exposure, as well as engaging with industry to develop and

---

[1] CBRN agents have the potential to cause widespread illness and death.

[2] Medical countermeasures for CBRN agents include drugs, biologics—such as vaccines—and devices to diagnose, treat, prevent, or mitigate potential effects of exposure. This report focuses on drugs and biologics.

[3] National Commission on Children and Disasters, *2010 Report to the President and Congress* (Rockville, Md.: October 2010). For the purpose of this report, "adults" are individuals 18 years of age and older, and the terms "children" and "pediatric population" are equivalent and refer to individuals younger than 18 years of age. The Food and Drug Administration (FDA) generally defines the pediatric population as individuals younger than 16 years of age, but relevant research has included children as old as 18.

GAO-13-438 Pediatric Medical Countermeasures

acquire the countermeasures.[4] Because desired CBRN medical countermeasures may not be developed to a point where they are available for acquisition, HHS's responsibility extends to overseeing and supporting research, as well as the development of these countermeasures by manufacturers. In 2006, HHS established the Public Health Emergency Medical Countermeasures Enterprise (PHEMCE), a federal interagency body that includes various HHS agencies and offices, as well as other federal departments, to provide recommendations to the Secretary of HHS on medical countermeasure priorities and development and acquisition activities. HHS's Centers for Disease Control and Prevention (CDC) manages the U.S. Strategic National Stockpile (SNS)—the national repository of medications, medical supplies, and equipment for HHS's use in mitigating the potential effects of exposure to CBRN agents and other public health emergencies. PHEMCE annually reviews the contents of the SNS to help HHS prioritize the maintenance and acquisition of medical countermeasures. CDC is responsible for distributing medical countermeasures from the SNS to states. In most instances, states are in turn responsible for distributing the countermeasures to local governments to dispense to affected populations. In addition, HHS's Food and Drug Administration (FDA) reviews safety, efficacy, and product quality data on medical countermeasures and approves, licenses, or clears them for specific indications and for use by various populations, including children.

You raised questions concerning pediatric medical countermeasures that are available in HHS's SNS, as well as medical and public health preparedness and response activities that are in place at the federal, state, and local levels to address the needs of the pediatric population in the event of a CBRN incident. This report addresses (1) the percentage of CBRN medical countermeasures in the SNS that are approved for pediatric use; (2) the challenges HHS faces in developing and acquiring CBRN medical countermeasures for the pediatric population, and the steps it is taking to address them; and (3) the ways that HHS has addressed the dispensing of pediatric medical countermeasures in its emergency response plans and guidance, and ways that state and local governments have addressed this issue.

---

[4]For the purposes of this report, we are using the term "industry" to include small research companies and manufacturing companies, both of which support HHS in efforts to research and develop CBRN medical countermeasures.

To determine the percentage of CBRN medical countermeasures in the SNS that are approved for pediatric use, we reviewed and analyzed HHS documentation, such as the PHEMCE annual reviews of the contents in the SNS, and determined that the information was sufficiently reliable.[5] We interviewed officials from the HHS agencies and offices that are responsible for CBRN emergency preparedness—including the Office of the Assistant Secretary for Preparedness and Response (ASPR), the Biomedical Advanced Research and Development Authority (BARDA), the National Institutes of Health (NIH), CDC, FDA, the Children's HHS Interagency Leadership on Disasters (CHILD) Working Group, as well as officials from PHEMCE. We also analyzed BARDA and CDC reports on their investments and interviewed HHS officials.[6]

To identify challenges that HHS faces in developing and acquiring CBRN medical countermeasures for the pediatric population and steps it is taking to address those challenges, we reviewed relevant laws, our earlier reports,[7] HHS documents, and other reports and information from subject-matter experts on emergency preparedness and pediatric health. We also interviewed officials from ASPR, BARDA, CDC, FDA, NIH, and PHEMCE, as well as industry officials and other expert groups, such as the American Academy of Pediatrics, Trust for America's Health, the Center for Infectious Disease Research and Policy, and state and local organizations, such as the Association of State and Territorial Health Officials and the National Association of County and City Health Officials.

To determine the ways that HHS has addressed the dispensing of pediatric medical countermeasures in its emergency response plans and guidance, and to assess how state and local governments have

---

[5]We reviewed supporting documentation provided by PHEMCE that included the list of CBRN medical countermeasures in the SNS as well as its analysis of whether each countermeasure was approved for all children, some children, or no children.

[6]For the purposes of this report, we used the term "investments" to mean obligations.

[7]GAO, *National Preparedness: Improvements Needed for Acquiring Medical Countermeasures to Threats from Terrorism and Other Sources*, GAO-12-121 (Washington, D.C.: Oct. 26, 2011), *National Preparedness: DHS and HHS Can Further Strengthen Coordination for Chemical, Biological, Radiological, and Nuclear Risk Assessments*, GAO-11-606 (Washington, D.C.: June 21, 2011), *Public Health Preparedness: Developing and Acquiring Medical Countermeasures Against Chemical, Biological, Radiological, and Nuclear Agents*, GAO-11-567T (Washington, D.C.: Apr. 13, 2011).

addressed pediatric dispensing, we reviewed HHS documents, such as the department's 12 emergency response plans for specific CBRN threats and CDC's emergency operations plan and guidance on dispensing medical countermeasures. In addition, we reviewed a sample of emergency response plans[8] from seven states and seven local governments to assess how state and local governments address pediatric dispensing.[9] Our findings related to the documentation and responses from the state and local governments are for illustrative purposes only and are not generalizable to other state and local governments' emergency response plans. We interviewed HHS and CDC officials responsible for addressing information in emergency response plans and providing guidance to state and local governments on dispensing pediatric medical countermeasures. We also interviewed state and local health officials and interest groups, such as the Association of State and Territorial Health Officials and the National Association of County and City Health Officials, to confirm our understanding about how dispensing CBRN medical countermeasures to children is handled during emergencies.

We conducted this performance audit from July 2012 through March 2013 in accordance with generally accepted government auditing standards. Those standards require that we plan and perform the audit to obtain sufficient, appropriate evidence to provide a reasonable basis for our findings and conclusions based on our audit objectives. We believe that the evidence obtained provides a reasonable basis for our findings and conclusions based on our audit objectives.

---

[8]For the purposes of this report, we are using the term "emergency response plan" to include any document a state or local government provided to us that describes an approach for responding to, or is used in the event of, an emergency.

[9]For the states, we received and reviewed emergency response plans from Arkansas, Michigan, Missouri, Oklahoma, Washington, and West Virginia, selected by a stratified random sample of the states, based on population size. We also received and reviewed documents from Virginia, although it was not part of the original sample. For local governments, we received and reviewed emergency response plans from Chicago (Illinois), Fresno (California), Milwaukee (Wisconsin), Nashville and Memphis (Tennessee), New York City (New York), and Virginia Beach (Virginia), selected by a stratified random sample of local governments that participate in CDC's Cities Readiness Initiative, based on the Census regions.

Background

Since the terrorist attacks of 2001, HHS has worked to prepare for and mitigate potential consequences resulting from the intentional or unintentional release of CBRN agents. This work has involved the efforts of various agencies, industry, and subject-matter experts to develop, acquire, and store medical countermeasures.

The development of medical countermeasures generally begins with research on able-bodied adults, according to the National Commission on Children and Disasters.[10] However, children have unique anatomical, physiological, and psychological differences that can predispose them in some circumstances to more serious or different adverse effects during public health emergencies compared to adults. HHS classifies children as part of the "at-risk population" and evaluates CBRN medical countermeasures for this group after developing them for the general adult population.[11] The at-risk population generally has unique characteristics that may interfere with an individual's ability to access or receive medical countermeasures. For example, individuals who have a limited ability to receive or respond to information because of hearing, vision, speech, or cognitive limitations would need to have information provided in such a way that they could understand it. In addition, before, during, and after an emergency, individuals may lose the support of caregivers, family, or friends. If separated from their caregivers, young children may be unable to identify themselves, and may lack the cognitive ability to assess situations and react appropriately. The National Commission on Children and Disasters and other experts in the field of pediatrics and emergency preparedness have reported that a disparity exists in the quality of adult and pediatric emergency care, especially in HHS's efforts to acquire FDA-approved pediatric medical countermeasures.[12]

---

[10]National Commission on Children and Disasters, *2010 Report to the President and Congress*.

[11]In addition to those individuals specifically recognized as "at-risk individuals" in the Pandemic and All-Hazards Preparedness Act of 2006—children, senior citizens, and pregnant women—individuals who may need additional response assistance include those who have disabilities, live in institutionalized settings, are from diverse cultures, have limited English proficiency or are non-English speaking, are transportation disadvantaged, have chronic medical disorders, or have pharmacological dependency.

[12]Institute of Medicine, *Safe and Effective Medicines for Children: Pediatric Studies Conducted Under the Best Pharmaceuticals for Children Act and the Pediatric Research Equity Act* (Washington, D.C.: The National Academies Press, 2012).

| Roles and Responsibilities of HHS's Agencies and Offices | HHS leads the federal public health and medical response to potential CBRN incidents, including identifying needed medical countermeasures to prevent or mitigate potential health effects from exposure and engaging with industry to develop and acquire the countermeasures. The following agencies and offices within HHS have responsibilities related to medical countermeasures. |

- ASPR is responsible for leading federal government efforts to research, develop, evaluate, and acquire medical countermeasures to diagnose, prevent, treat, or mitigate the potential health effects from exposure to CBRN agents. Within ASPR, BARDA, which was established by the Pandemic and All-Hazards Preparedness Act of 2006, is responsible for overseeing and funding advanced development and acquisition of CBRN medical countermeasures.

- NIH is responsible for conducting and coordinating basic and applied research to develop new or enhanced medical countermeasures for CBRN agents.

- FDA is responsible for regulating the development and approval of drugs, biologics, diagnostics, and devices, which includes assessing the safety, efficacy, and quality of CBRN medical countermeasures before approval and postmarket.

- CDC is responsible for maintaining the SNS and supporting state and local public health departments in their efforts to respond to public health emergencies, including providing guidance and recommendations for the mass distribution and use of medical countermeasures.

| CBRN Threats and Medical Countermeasures | Since 2004, the Department of Homeland Security (DHS), in consultation with the Secretary of HHS, has determined that certain CBRN agents pose a threat to the nation that could affect national security.[13] HHS has used these material threat determinations to assess the potential public |

---

[13]Pub. L. No. 108-276. § 3(a)(2), 118 Stat. 835, 844 (2004). The Project BioShield Act of 2004 calls for HHS to assess the public health consequences of exposure to those CBRN agents that the Department of Homeland Security, in consultation with the Secretary of HHS, determines are material threats to the nation and to determine for which of these agents medical countermeasures are necessary to protect the public health. 42 U.S.C. § 247d-6b(c)(2).

health and medical consequences of the CBRN agents, and to establish specific medical requirements for developing countermeasures. Assessing the medical consequences and establishing medical requirements are both interim steps in determining the types and quantities of medical countermeasures required to respond to the agents.

CBRN agents differ from one another in their potential to cause widespread illness and death. In the event of a release of a CBRN agent, medical countermeasures may be needed for rapid diagnosis, treatment, and prevention of infection, illness, and injury, but the dose and formulation of the countermeasures needed for an individual may vary according to traits such as the individual's age and weight, especially when considering the needs of children.[14] For example, in some cases, it is desirable to have multiple formulations of countermeasures available— such as oral liquid suspensions and tablets—to facilitate patient compliance. There are an increasing number of available medical countermeasures to protect the nation against CBRN agents. Supplies of countermeasures that are available are generally held in the SNS for use in a public health emergency. The SNS is designed to supplement and resupply state and local public health departments in the event of a national public health emergency such as a CBRN incident.[15]

To acquire medical countermeasures for use during a CBRN incident where there is a lack of a significant commercial market, Congress authorized the appropriation of approximately $5.6 billion and the use of a Special Reserve Fund for the procurement of certain countermeasures.[16] The Special Reserve Fund has been used to acquire CBRN medical

---

[14]For example, the palatability of a mixture made by crushing solid oral doses of a drug into a food or liquid may need to be addressed for pediatric formulations. Palatability refers to the taste, texture, and smell of a medication, and is considered in the development of pediatric formulations.

[15]Many state and local jurisdictions have purchased their own supplies of CBRN medical countermeasures, such as ciprofloxacin and doxycycline, to be better prepared to respond to public health emergencies. These stockpiles are typically created to ensure early access to medicines to protect first responders, among others, so that these essential employees can quickly respond to the emergency.

[16]The 2004 DHS Appropriations Act appropriated approximately $5.6 billion for biodefense countermeasures to remain available until 2013. Pub. L. No. 108-90, 117 Stat. 1137, 1148 (2003). The Project Bioshield Act defined the Special Reserve Fund for purposes of the countermeasures program to include the Biodefense Countermeasures appropriations account. Pub. L. No. 108-276, 118 Stat. 852.

countermeasures for the SNS. The Pandemic and All-Hazards Preparedness Reauthorization Act of 2013 reauthorizes the Special Reserve Fund and authorizes $2.8 billion over 5 years, from fiscal year 2014 through fiscal year 2018.[17]

FDA Approval and Emergency Authorization of Medical Countermeasures

In general, drugs, devices, diagnostics, and biologics such as vaccines, including CBRN countermeasures, cannot be marketed legally in the United States without FDA approval. To approve a countermeasure, FDA requires manufacturers to sufficiently demonstrate the safety, efficacy, and product quality of the countermeasure for the intended indication and population specified in the application.[18] When products are approved, clinicians might prescribe them for unapproved indications or to unapproved populations, also referred to as "off-label use." Generally, a doctor-patient relationship should exist for off-label dispensing of a medical countermeasure. In a CBRN incident, dispensing of countermeasures for approved or off-label indications may have to occur outside of the doctor-patient relationship.[19] According to HHS, many medicines and vaccines used in normal, standard medical care for the pediatric population are prescribed using this off-label practice. However, one possible consequence of off-label use of countermeasures by children is that some children, depending on weight or growth rates, may not receive the most appropriate dose of a medical countermeasure. In addition, some children may be at risk for side effects that are unique to

[17]Pub. L. No. 113-5, title IV, 127 Stat. 161, 193-195 (2013). An authorization of appropriations does not constitute an appropriation of public funds. Normally, an authorization of appropriations legislation is a prerequisite for making appropriations for the given programs or agencies.

[18]FDA requires drug companies, also known as drug manufacturers, to specify in their applications for government approval of a product the indication intended for their products' use. The indication generally describes the disease, condition, or symptoms that the drug is intended to treat, prevent, mitigate, cure, or diagnose, as well as the populations for which the manufacturer has conducted testing and for which it is seeking approval.

[19]Medical countermeasure dispensing provides medical countermeasures in support of treatment or prophylaxis (oral or vaccination) to the identified population in accordance with public health guidelines and recommendations.

children, including adverse effects on their growth and development.[20] To encourage the study of more drugs for pediatric use, Congress passed the Best Pharmaceuticals for Children Act in 2002, which provides financial incentives to product sponsors, and the Pediatric Research Equity Act of 2003. These laws encourage or require product sponsors to conduct pediatric studies, and also include labeling requirements, including labeling updates that result from pediatric drug studies.[21]

Although FDA regulates the use of medical countermeasures by approving their use by specific populations and for specific indications, during a public health emergency—such as a CBRN incident—FDA can authorize the use of those countermeasures by populations or for indications for which they have not been approved. This can occur in one of two ways. First, FDA can authorize the use of countermeasures that are unapproved, or approved but for a different indication, in a declared emergency to diagnose, treat, or prevent serious or life-threatening diseases or conditions caused by CBRN agents, when there are no adequate, approved, and available alternatives, and other criteria are met.[22] This is referred to as an Emergency Use Authorization (EUA). In order for FDA to authorize the emergency use of a countermeasure, it must be reasonable to believe that, based on the evidence available, the product may be effective in diagnosing, treating, or preventing such

---

[20]The Public Readiness and Emergency Preparedness Act provides compensation to individuals for serious physical injuries or deaths from countermeasures identified in a declaration of a public health emergency issued by the Secretary of HHS. The act authorizes HHS to issue a declaration that provides immunity from tort liability—except for willful misconduct—to certain individuals and organizations involved in the development, manufacture, distribution, administration, and use of these countermeasures. Pub. L. No. 109-148, division C, 119 Stat. 2680, 2818-2832 (2005) (codified at 42 U.S.C. § 247d-6d).

[21]The Best Pharmaceuticals for Children Act offers drug sponsors—typically manufacturers—incentives to conduct pediatric studies, such as by extending the company's market exclusivity for that product for 6 months. Protection from competition under market exclusivity can include the marketing of a generic copy. Pub. L. No. 107-109, 115 Stat. 1408 (2002). The Pediatric Research Equity Act allows FDA to require manufacturers of drugs and biological products to submit pediatric testing data at the time of new drug applications. Pub. L. No. 108-155, 117 Stat. 1936 (2003). Both acts were extended in 2007 and are now permanent in the Food and Drug Administration Safety and Innovation Act of 2012. Pub. L. No. 110-85, §§ 401-404, 501-503, 121 Stat. 823, 866-890 (2007); Pub. L. No. 112-144, § 501, 126 Stat. 993, 1039-1040 (2012) (pertinent provisions codified as amended at 21 U.S.C. §§ 355a, 355c).

[22]See 21 U.S.C. § 360bbb-3. The Secretary of HHS has delegated authority to make such determinations to the Commissioner of FDA.

disease or condition. In addition, the known and potential benefits of the product must outweigh the known and potential risks.[23]

Second, if a countermeasure's safety and efficacy are not sufficiently documented, FDA may allow its use under an Investigational New Drug (IND) application, which allows for expanded access to medical countermeasures during an emergency[24] while the safety and efficacy are being investigated. In order for children to receive investigational medical countermeasures under an IND, written, informed consent is required. Documentation of informed consent is not required when children receive countermeasures through an EUA; however, to the extent practicable given the circumstances of the emergency, patients are to be informed about the known and potential benefits and risks of the countermeasure and the right to refuse the countermeasure.

Medical Countermeasure Research, Development, Acquisition, and Support

HHS's and PHEMCE's medical countermeasure acquisition strategy is based on a multistep process. This process includes assessing the threat and public health consequences of CBRN agents, determining the type and quantity of needed medical countermeasures, evaluating the public health response capability, and developing and acquiring countermeasures against CBRN agents for the SNS. Because desired CBRN medical countermeasures may not be developed to a point where they are available for acquisition, HHS oversees and supports research and development of these countermeasures. (See fig. 1.) NIH and BARDA oversee and support CBRN medical countermeasure research and development, which is conducted in several stages: (1) basic research, (2) applied research, (3) early development, and (4) advanced development.[25] NIH typically provides federal funding to academic

---

[23]If state or local governments dispense countermeasures in a manner that is inconsistent with the terms of an EUA, their liability protections afforded by the Public Readiness and Emergency Preparedness Act may be affected.

[24]21 U.S.C. § 360bbb. The Secretary of HHS has delegated authority to make such determinations to the Commissioner of FDA. While INDs may be submitted for a variety of purposes, in this report we use the term IND to refer to only those submitted for expanded access to medical countermeasures during an emergency.

[25]In addition to approving or licensing medical countermeasures, FDA works with researchers throughout the development stages to review safety and efficacy test results and provide technical assistance to help ensure that research meets FDA's regulatory requirements.

centers and small biotechnology companies for basic and applied research and early development.[26] Once an organization's research is at the advanced development stage and moving toward the development of a product that will meet HHS's specific requirements, it may partner with an established pharmaceutical or manufacturing company to continue the advanced development. Within HHS, the product transitions from NIH to BARDA to support its advanced development.[27] If a countermeasure is not FDA-approved or licensed, its acquisition into the SNS is typically funded by the Project BioShield Special Reserve Fund.[28] If a countermeasure is FDA-approved or licensed, CDC generally purchases the countermeasure for the SNS.

---

[26]Early, or basic, research is intended to better understand CBRN agents and the response of the host organism to the agents through the study of the cellular and molecular biology of agents and hosts, their physiological processes, and their genome sequences and structures. Applied, or translational, research builds on basic research by validating and testing concepts in practical settings to identify potential products. Successful concepts move from the applied research stage into the early development stage, in order to demonstrate basic safety, reproducibility, and ability to be used in humans.

[27]In the advanced development stage, potential medical countermeasures are further evaluated to demonstrate safety and efficacy for preventing, diagnosing, or treating disease. Successful products are then available for development and acquisition. In addition, BARDA determines that manufacturing, scale-up production, and licensing of countermeasures can be achieved in a timely and reliable manner.

[28]The Project BioShield Act of 2004 provides that the Special Reserve Fund may be used to acquire countermeasures for which the HHS Secretary determines that sufficient and satisfactory clinical experience or research data support a reasonable conclusion that the product will qualify for FDA approval or licensing within 8 years. In 2013, the Pandemic and All-Hazards Preparedness and Reauthorization Act extended the timeline for acquisitions, allowing for the use of the Special Reserve Fund to acquire countermeasures for which the HHS Secretary determines that sufficient and satisfactory clinical experience or research data support a reasonable conclusion that the product will qualify for FDA approval or licensing within 10 years. 42 U.S.C. § 247d-6b(c)(1)(B)(i)(III)(bb).

Figure 1: Processes for Medical Countermeasure Development and Acquisition

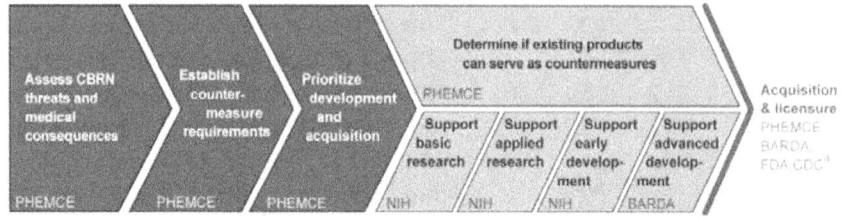

☐ Processes for countermeasure priority setting

☐ Processes for countermeasure development and acquisition

BARDA: Biomedical Advanced Research and Development Authority

CBRN: chemical, biological, radiological, and nuclear

CDC: Centers for Disease Control and Prevention

FDA: Food and Drug Administration

NIH: National Institutes of Health

PHEMCE: Public Health Emergency Medical Countermeasures Enterprise

Source: GAO analysis of Department of Health and Human Services information.

[a]In addition to approving, licensing, or clearing medical countermeasures, FDA works with researchers throughout the development stages to review safety and efficacy test results and provide technical assistance to help ensure that research meets FDA's regulatory requirements.

Planning for Medical Countermeasure Distribution and Dispensing

Public health emergency response planning for CBRN incidents requires efforts at the federal, state, and local levels. Governments at each level have developed emergency response plans that outline their respective responsibilities during public health emergencies, which include responsibilities for distributing and dispensing medical countermeasures to the public. The federal government is responsible for planning the federal response to CBRN incidents. HHS has developed response plans for specific CBRN agents to help coordinate the federal response to such emergencies.[29] Federal assistance to state and local governments would

---

[29]HHS has developed 12 response plans to address CBRN incidents as of December 2012: 8 are For Official Use Only, and 4 are publicly available. Officials told us there are fewer publicly available plans than For Official Use Only plans because some plans are currently in draft form and will be available in public versions once they have been cleared by HHS for release. The For Official Use Only response plans address some chemical (nerve agent, blister agent, and chlorine tank explosion), biological (pneumonic plague, botulism food contamination, and aerosolized anthrax), radiological (radiological dispersal device), and nuclear (improvised nuclear device) incidents. The publicly available response plans address biological (botulinum food contamination and aerosolized anthrax), radiological (radiological dispersal device), and nuclear (nuclear detonation) incidents.

GAO-13-438 Pediatric Medical Countermeasures

be provided if resources were unavailable or if state and local governments were overwhelmed and requested public health or medical assistance from the federal government. HHS would then direct CDC to distribute medical countermeasures from the SNS to the states.

Once CDC distributes medical countermeasures from the SNS to a state, in most instances the state then distributes the countermeasures to local governments, based on established plans. State and local governments are responsible for developing plans for receiving, distributing, and dispensing medical countermeasures from the SNS. These plans are intended to describe all functions that are required to accomplish these tasks, in order to get medical countermeasures to the affected population as quickly and efficiently as possible. Some states plan to receive countermeasures and immediately turn them over to a local jurisdiction for staging, distributing, and dispensing during an emergency. Other states plan to receive medical countermeasures at a state warehouse facility and then deliver them directly to points of dispensing (POD) or hospitals. Each state is responsible for determining the best method for its circumstances and resources. Local governments, in turn, are responsible for receiving and dispensing medical countermeasures in a timely and efficient manner.

More than Half of CBRN Medical Countermeasures Have Been Approved for at Least Some Children

About 60 percent of CBRN medical countermeasures in the SNS have been approved for children, but in many instances approval is limited to specific age groups. Specifically, PHEMCE officials stated that about 38 percent of the CBRN medical countermeasures in the SNS have been approved for children of all ages for treatment of certain CBRN threats. For example, ciprofloxacin and doxycycline as antimicrobials indicated for postexposure prophylaxis of inhalational anthrax, atropine as a treatment for exposure to nerve gas, and raxibacumab as an anthrax antitoxin have all been approved for use in the pediatric population for these indications. In addition, 22 percent of the CBRN medical countermeasures in the SNS have been approved for use by some, but not all, pediatric age groups for treatment of certain CBRN threats. For example, Prussian blue—a medical countermeasure that removes certain internalized radiological particles from the body—is approved for children ages 2 and above for that indication, but has not been approved for those less than 2 years of age. PHEMCE officials stated that the remaining 40 percent of the CBRN countermeasures have not been approved for any pediatric use.[30] For example, anthrax vaccine adsorbed (AVA) has not been approved for use by any children.[31] Furthermore, some of the CBRN medical countermeasures in the SNS have not been approved to treat individuals of any age for the specific indications for which they have been stockpiled. For example, ciprofloxacin is stockpiled in the SNS for the treatment of anthrax, plague, and tularemia, but is not approved for these indications. It is, however, approved for postexposure prophylaxis of inhalational anthrax in all age groups. In addition, for certain CBRN threats, there are no countermeasures available in the SNS because treatments for the conditions do not exist beyond supportive care.

According to HHS officials, almost all medical countermeasures in the SNS can be used by children in an emergency if already approved for children or if FDA authorizes their use through an EUA or if an IND protocol is in effect. Even products that are not approved for a CBRN indication may be used in a public health emergency under an EUA—after an emergency has been declared—or under an IND protocol. HHS officials told us that almost all medical countermeasures that are not approved for use by the pediatric population can be used in an emergency under an EUA. However, some countermeasures, such as AVA vaccine, lack sufficient data to support their use by the pediatric population under an EUA. This vaccine would need to be administered to the pediatric population under an IND protocol. HHS officials explained that two different IND protocols for AVA have been developed in preparation for a potential anthrax-related public health emergency. The first protocol is designed to provide children access to the vaccine. It would require parents or guardians to sign consent forms to allow their

---

[30]According to members of PHEMCE, these percentages were derived from an analysis of the regulatory status of the contents of the SNS performed in June 2012. However, these percentages may not entirely reflect the availability of countermeasures to be used by children because three items that were counted as not approved for use by children are therapeutic ointments that are not labeled by age. An official from PHEMCE stated that therapeutic ointments are assumed to be safe for use by children unless there is a warning against their use.

[31]In March 2013, the Presidential Commission for the Study of Bioethical Issues reported that the federal government would have to take multiple steps, including minimal-risk research with adult volunteers, before considering pediatric clinical trials to test the safety and efficacy of AVA in children. The Presidential Commission for the Study of Bioethical Issues, *Safeguarding Children: Pediatric Medical Countermeasure Research* (Washington, D.C.: March 2013).

children to receive anthrax vaccine during an emergency. The second IND protocol would require parents or guardians to sign consent forms to allow their children to participate in a research study after receiving the vaccine.[32] (See app. I for additional information on the regulatory status of types of CBRN medical countermeasures in the SNS for the pediatric population.)

Although HHS can provide information on the proportion of SNS countermeasures that can be used by children, it cannot provide information on the funds invested in procuring these countermeasures. HHS does not separately track the funds that it has invested in the acquisition and development of pediatric medical countermeasures because it does not account separately for investments related to the different populations. HHS procures CBRN medical countermeasures for the SNS based on, among other things, the list of material threats to the nation, public health response and medical consequence assessments, and available resources. Since 2004, BARDA has invested over $4 billion of Project BioShield's Special Reserve Fund, which supports advanced development and manufacturing of potential CBRN medical countermeasures, in contracts to support medical countermeasure development in healthy and at-risk populations, including the pediatric population. In addition, between 2009 and 2012, CDC's budget to maintain or acquire licensed CBRN medical countermeasures for the SNS was over $1.5 billion; however, no funds were specifically designated exclusively for products to be used only by the pediatric population.

---

[32]HHS officials stated that under this second IND protocol, parents would consent to having blood drawn from their children when the vaccine was administered during an emergency, as well as submitting other health information about their children after they were vaccinated in order to follow up on the safety of the vaccine in children. Officials stated that these actions could provide FDA with some safety and immunogenicity data to inform use of the vaccine in children in future emergencies. Officials emphasized that if there are no data available in advance of public health emergencies, the gaps in the data could be addressed only during an actual event.

HHS Faces Challenges in Developing and Acquiring Pediatric Medical Countermeasures but Is Taking Steps to Address the Needs of the Pediatric Population

HHS faces economic, regulatory, scientific, and ethical challenges in its efforts to develop and acquire CBRN medical countermeasures for children in an emergency. Despite these challenges, HHS is taking steps to focus on the pediatric population and develop pediatric formulations of existing medical countermeasures.

HHS Faces Economic, Regulatory, Scientific, and Ethical Challenges in Developing and Acquiring Pediatric Medical Countermeasures

HHS faces a variety of interrelated challenges in developing and acquiring pediatric CBRN medical countermeasures, including economic, regulatory, scientific, and ethical issues that impede the ability of HHS to address the needs of children during a CBRN incident.[33] Economic challenges facing HHS include the high failure rate of research, development, approval, and licensure of most drugs, vaccines, and diagnostic devices. Agency and industry officials told us that the risk of failure in developing countermeasures for children is even higher than the risk in developing them for the adult population. This risk, as well as a lack of a commercial market for most CBRN medical countermeasures, has made it difficult for HHS to attract companies willing to invest in such development and has therefore impeded HHS's ability to acquire the needed countermeasures. In addition, various reports have stated that insufficient economic incentives are available to encourage the private sector to invest millions of dollars to develop potential new pediatric

[33]These challenges have been described in past GAO reports, various HHS reports, and reports by subject-matter experts. See GAO-12-121, GAO-11-606, and GAO-11-567T. See also Department of Health and Human Services, *The Children's HHS Interagency Leadership on Disasters (CHILD) Working Group: Summary of Recommendations and Implementation Efforts* (April 2012); National Commission on Children and Disasters, *2010 Report to the President and Congress.*

medical countermeasures.[34] According to CDC officials, while it is desirable to have oral liquid formulations available for young children who cannot swallow pills, it is not always practical to develop and acquire them for the SNS because such countermeasures for children can be more costly to procure and maintain, have shorter shelf lives, and may exceed manufacturer capability, as opposed to alternatives such as pill crushing and mixing that can be explored for all but the youngest children. CDC estimated that it would cost approximately $3 billion to purchase sufficient quantities of oral liquid formulations of countermeasures for the SNS to support the needs of all children—an amount well over CDC's approximately $600 million annual budget for CBRN medical countermeasures over the past 5 years. Further, because the shelf life of liquids is shorter than that of tablets, oral liquid formulations would require more frequent investments. Finally, even if such funds were available, the manufacturing capacity to meet such acquisition requests may not be available.

The FDA regulatory pathway for developing pediatric CBRN medical countermeasures also poses unique challenges making it more difficult than for adult countermeasures. The Institute of Medicine, the National Biodefense Science Board, HHS, and FDA have stated that it is difficult to meet FDA's requirements for data from adequate and well-controlled clinical investigations to support the approval of pediatric medical countermeasures because large, complex clinical trials are needed to prove safety and efficacy. As a result of this regulatory challenge, FDA has increasingly relied on alternative sources of data in order to approve, license, or authorize the use of medical countermeasures by children. For example, FDA allows researchers to submit evidence of efficacy obtained from historical inferences and appropriate studies in animals in accordance with FDA's Animal Rule.[35] Another challenge to developing

---

[34]Institute of Medicine, *Advancing Regulatory Science for Medical Countermeasure Development* (National Academy of Sciences: 2010); National Biodefense Science Board, *Where Are the Countermeasures? Protecting America's Health from CBRN Threats* (2010); Department of Health and Human Services, *The Children's HHS Interagency Leadership on Disasters (CHILD) Working Group: Summary of Recommendations and Implementation Efforts*.

[35]21 C.F.R. §§ 314.600-650; 601.90-.95. The Animal Rule states that when it is neither ethical nor feasible to conduct human efficacy studies, FDA may grant marketing approval of CBRN countermeasures based on adequate and well-controlled animal studies when the results of those studies establish that the drug or biological product is reasonably likely to produce clinical benefit in humans.

countermeasures for children is that manufacturers are permitted, under certain circumstances, to avoid testing drugs for use by children. For example, manufacturers of CBRN countermeasures often seek an orphan drug designation for a new countermeasure,[36] which, if granted, exempts the manufacturer from the requirement to conduct pediatric studies under the Pediatric Research Equity Act.[37]

There are scientific challenges in obtaining sufficient pediatric safety and efficacy information to appropriately inform the use of CBRN medical countermeasures for children. For example, FDA officials told us that extrapolating data to support efficacy information on a medical countermeasure from animal studies presents not only regulatory, but also complex scientific challenges to understanding how children would react to exposure to CBRN agents. NIH and industry officials told us that exposure in juvenile animal models is also not well understood. For example, extrapolating data from animal studies presents other scientific challenges in understanding the response to the medical countermeasures used to prevent or treat the disease or condition. Appropriate animal models have not yet been developed for many CBRN agents. In addition, the presentation of the disease or condition that humans manifest following exposure to a CBRN agent may not be the same as that for animals following exposure to the same CBRN agent, thus complicating the task of researchers that are relying on animal models. Further, there is an initial hurdle of extrapolating data from animal models for adults first; only after those data have been extrapolated and applied to the adult population can researchers extrapolate to children. For example, in order to develop or indicate a countermeasure for use in children, scientists generally take an existing countermeasure that has

---

[36]A drug may receive an orphan designation if it is intended for conditions or diseases that affect fewer than 200,000 persons in the United States. CBRN and non-CBRN drugs that qualify and receive orphan designation are exempt from pediatric research requirements under the Pediatric Research Equity Act. Orphan designation qualifies the sponsor of the product for the tax credit and marketing incentives of the Orphan Drug Act. See Pub. L. No. 97-414, 96 Stat. 2049 (1983) (codified at 21 U.S.C. §§ 360aa-360cc; 26 U.S.C. § 45C).

[37]Until 1997, most drugs used to treat children were tested for safety and efficacy only in adults. The Pediatric Research Equity Act of 2003 requires assessments of safety and efficacy of drugs and biological products for pediatric use for the indication for which they are approved in the adult population. HHS may grant deferrals and full or partial waivers from these requirements. Products with an orphan drug designation for a rare disease or condition are exempt from the requirements of the Pediatric Research Equity Act.

already been developed for adults and then adjust certain variables such as weight-based dosing and delivery mechanisms to test the safety and efficacy of the countermeasure in children. This is not straightforward because children may have special susceptibilities to the CBRN agent and special age- and weight-dependent responses to the medical countermeasures.

Finally, HHS faces ethical challenges in its efforts to develop and acquire pediatric medical countermeasures because, absent a CBRN event, it is generally not ethical or feasible to obtain dosing, safety, and efficacy data for children when there is no potential direct benefit to them in the context of a clinical trial. FDA-regulated clinical trials that include children as subjects must consider both the risks to which a child may be exposed in a clinical investigation and whether the proposed intervention offers a prospect of direct benefit to the child.[38] Because children can be enrolled as subjects in research only when directly necessary and when the research is ethically sound, industry officials we met with stated that researching CBRN medical countermeasures' effect on children is nearly impossible. Industry officials told us that knowing that CBRN medical countermeasure research has a clear, direct benefit to a child participating in a study would always be unlikely because diseases caused by CBRN agents do not generally occur naturally.

HHS Is Taking Steps to Focus on the Pediatric Population and Develop Pediatric Formulations of Existing Medical Countermeasures

Although challenges persist in developing and acquiring pediatric medical countermeasures, HHS is beginning to address gaps in the SNS for pediatric medical countermeasures by focusing agency efforts on children, developing pediatric formulations of medical countermeasures in the SNS, and preparing and reviewing EUA and IND application materials in advance of emergencies.

Focusing Department-wide Efforts

HHS is taking steps to focus department-wide efforts on children's CBRN medical countermeasure needs. In 2010, FDA announced its Medical Countermeasures Initiative, which is intended to foster the development and availability of medical countermeasures, including those intended to

---

[38]21 C.F.R. part 50, subpart D (Additional Safeguards for Children in Clinical Investigations).

GAO-13-438 Pediatric Medical Countermeasures

be used by children.[39] FDA officials said the initiative has improved the regulatory pathway for advancing the development and acquisition of medical countermeasures, for example, by clarifying and streamlining its review process and countermeasure requirements, which may entice manufacturers to develop new, novel medical countermeasures, including countermeasures with pediatric applicability. In addition, in 2010, HHS increased its focus on children's needs with the establishment of the CHILD Working Group, which was formed to identify and integrate activities related to the needs of children across all HHS inter- and intragovernmental disaster planning activities and operations. The CHILD Working Group has developed recommendations for how HHS can improve the delivery of care to children who are affected by disasters. In 2011, in the area of medical countermeasures, the CHILD Working Group recommended that HHS provide clarity in the regulatory pathway for pediatric medical countermeasures; obtain the appropriate data, when available, to provide clinical pediatric dosing and use guidance for existing medical countermeasures; and gather safety and efficacy data from nontraditional sources to support the use of pediatric medical countermeasures under EUAs and for eventual FDA approval.[40]

According to HHS officials, many of the recommendations from the CHILD Working Group are being adopted by HHS. For example, in 2011, HHS developed the Pediatric Obstetric Integrated Program Team, which includes pediatric and obstetric subject-matter experts who advise PHEMCE on pediatric and obstetric medical countermeasure issues. This integrated program team is intended to recommend that pediatric medical countermeasure needs are consistently considered throughout the entire medical countermeasure development process and that pediatric subject-matter experts help consider complex ethical, scientific, and legal issues associated with studies that are necessary for the licensure and approval of medical countermeasures for children. In 2012 the integrated program team conducted a review of the contents of the SNS to determine the suitability of the contents for use by children, and it subsequently used the review to make recommendations to PHEMCE, and to petition for new

---

[39]The Medical Countermeasures Initiative is composed of three pillars that (1) enhance the medical countermeasure review process; (2) advance regulatory science for medical countermeasure development; and (3) optimize the legal and policy framework for approving medical countermeasures.

[40]Department of Health and Human Services, *2011 Report of the Children's HHS Interagency Leadership on Disasters (CHILD) Working Group: Progress and Future Directions* (January 2012).

medical countermeasure development. The content of the review is a work product of the integrated program team, and HHS has no plans to formally issue it. According to HHS, the findings and recommendations were considered during the 2012 SNS Annual Review. Further, in 2012, BARDA announced that where feasible and appropriate, it would be including development of medical countermeasures for the pediatric population as part of all base contracts moving forward.

Adapting Pediatric Formulations of Existing Medical Countermeasures

HHS has taken steps to support the development of CBRN medical countermeasure formulations for children, and has begun to base the pediatric dosing information on other evidence, such as by extrapolating from relevant and historical data of the countermeasure. Countermeasures are not approved for an indication unless data on the safety and efficacy of the countermeasure are available for a particular population, such as children. According to FDA officials, the agency has determined that in a smallpox emergency, the investigational smallpox vaccine under development may be authorized for use under an EUA in populations with compromised immune systems, including children. Specifically, in 2007 a second-generation smallpox vaccine, developed for persons determined to be at high risk for infection, was licensed based on data from clinical trials and the routine vaccination of infants in the United States through 1972. The vaccine was not studied in pediatric populations; however, this second-generation vaccine was similar to the vaccine that was routinely used to vaccinate infants in the United States through 1972 and had been demonstrated to be safe and effective in children. Therefore, FDA has determined that this vaccine could be used in pediatric populations under its license in a smallpox emergency. Similarly, pralidoxime chloride, prescribed as an antidote to treat nerve agent poisoning, has also been approved for use by children based on the extrapolation of efficacy data from both the adult and pediatric populations. In addition, FDA has used historical data from other countries to support EUAs or product approvals for pediatric indications when analogous U.S. data were neither available nor obtainable. For example, according to FDA officials, in 1987, a radiological incident in Brazil provided the majority of the pediatric data that FDA reviewed to assess the safety and efficacy of a radiological countermeasure. The data included the use of the countermeasure by both adults and children. The review allowed FDA to approve the countermeasure for children ages 2 and older in 2003.

PHEMCE has also encouraged adapting and manufacturing of oral liquid formulations of existing medical countermeasures in order to ease dispensing of countermeasures in the SNS for children. For example,

BARDA is contracting with industry partners to manufacture a liquid form of a countermeasure that removes certain radioactive particles from the body through the intestinal tract.[41] Additionally, PHEMCE is considering lowering the recommended age at which children should be administered oral liquid suspensions of doxycycline in lieu of crushed tablets. CDC officials told us that they would like to have more oral liquid suspensions considered for the SNS; however, PHEMCE officials have reported that crushing tablets would be an acceptable alternative and would have benefits for storage, dispensing, and dosing. As a result, FDA and CDC have developed instructions for crushing certain approved medical countermeasures for use by people who cannot swallow tablets or capsules. The crushing instructions include instructions for mixing the countermeasures with food or drink to make them more palatable to children. Crushing instructions generally include weight-based dosing instructions, the number of doses required per day, and instructions for how to crush pills and mix them.[42]

Preparing and Reviewing EUA and IND Materials in Advance of Emergencies

Relevant component agencies within HHS collaborate to prepare and review materials for EUAs and INDs in advance of public health emergencies to ensure that sufficient data are available to support authorizations for the use of certain medical countermeasures by children. According to CDC officials, the agency assesses, on a regular basis, the contents in the SNS and updates and assembles data and information for those countermeasures that are not approved for use by children so that in the event of a public health emergency, the contents can be disseminated to states quickly. Specifically, to prepare for such an emergency, CDC collaborates with BARDA, NIH, FDA, and manufacturers to develop the EUA and IND submissions in advance of an actual incident, so that all medical countermeasures in the SNS can be used by children. In addition, they consult with the American Academy of Pediatrics on pediatric issues.

---

[41]That countermeasure, Prussian blue, is currently licensed for adult and pediatric patients over 2 years of age.

[42]Department of Health and Human Services, Public Health Emergency Medical Countermeasures Enterprise, *Pediatric Medical Countermeasure Roundtable for National Health Security: Meeting Report* (Oct. 13-14, 2010). Some of the medical countermeasures being considered for crushing include Prussian blue, doxycycline, and ciprofloxacin.

GAO-13-438 Pediatric Medical Countermeasures

HHS and State and Local Governments Address Dispensing of Pediatric Medical Countermeasures in Their Response Plans

More than half of HHS's emergency response plans that we examined included information about pediatric medical countermeasures. CDC and FDA developed guidance on pediatric dispensing for state and local government use. The state and local plans we examined also provided details about dispensing to the pediatric population during an emergency.

More than Half of HHS's Response Plans We Reviewed Include Information about Dispensing Pediatric Medical Countermeasures

Of the 12 HHS CBRN response plans we reviewed, more than half included information about dispensing pediatric medical countermeasures. Specifically, 7 of these threat-specific plans contained information about medical countermeasures that could be dispensed for use by children in the event of a CBRN incident.[43] The type of information included varied by plan. For example, two of the plans for responding to biological threats identified preferred and alternative countermeasures, and the appropriate dosages, that should be dispensed to children during an event. For a chemical incident, one of the plans indicated a premedication that should be used in pediatric patients before intubating them.[44] The response plans for nuclear or radiological incidents also included information about medical countermeasures that could be used by children, although one plan noted that an EUA would be required before some of the countermeasures could be dispensed to the pediatric population. Although more than half of HHS's response plans included information about dispensing specific countermeasures to children, HHS officials told us that the purpose of these plans is to provide guidance for emergency responses at the federal level, and not instructions for use at the state and local level, which is where dispensing to children would

---

[43]Not all of the plans would necessarily include information about which specific medical countermeasure is to be dispensed to children during a CBRN incident, according to HHS officials. For example, treatment for exposure to certain CBRN agents sometimes only requires supportive care, rather than a specific medical countermeasure.

[44]Intubation is a medical procedure in which a tube is placed into the windpipe (trachea), through the mouth or the nose. In most emergency situations, it is placed through the mouth.

occur.[45] While these plans are intended primarily to support the federal response, they could also be used by state and local governments to inform their activities as part of planning their own response to a public health emergency.[46]

HHS officials told us that they were moving away from the use of separate, threat-specific response plans and were developing a single "all-hazards" response plan.[47] This all-hazards plan would include sections for responding to specific CBRN events. According to HHS officials, these sections would address pediatric dispensing, including EUA and IND requirements. Additionally, a briefing paper about the pediatric population in disasters would be included in the all-hazards plan.

CDC and FDA Guidance for State and Local Governments Includes Information on Pediatric Dispensing

Both CDC and FDA developed guidance for the dispensing of CBRN medical countermeasures from the SNS to the public, including children. For example, CDC developed guidance about receiving, distributing, and dispensing contents from the SNS to help state and local emergency management and public health personnel plan for the use of countermeasures from the SNS.[48] The guidance, which could be used as a reference document or as a checklist by local and state planners, referred to the pediatric population in multiple sections, including an appendix about pediatric dispensing considerations. For example, the guidance described how the color "pink" is used to identify pediatric supplies included in the SNS. Additionally, the appendix noted that the

---

[45]The federal government emergency responses are intended to provide support, resources, program implementation, and services that are most likely needed to save lives, protect property and the environment, restore essential services and critical infrastructure, and help victims and communities return to normal following domestic incidents. HHS is the primary agency responsible for efforts related to public health and medical services in order to provide the mechanism for coordinated federal assistance to supplement state, tribal, and local resources in response to an emergency.

[46]HHS also developed two web-based resources that can also be used to inform CBRN planning at other levels of government—the Chemical Hazards Emergency Medical Management and Radiation Emergency Medical Management guidance documents. See http://www.chemm.nlm.nih.gov/ and http://www.remm.nlm.gov/, respectively, accessed January 25, 2013.

[47]HHS officials said that they anticipate releasing this plan by August 2013.

[48]Centers for Disease Control and Prevention, *Receiving, Distributing, and Dispensing Strategic National Stockpile Assets: A Guide for Preparedness,* ver.10.02 (August 2006).

SNS has limited amounts of oral suspensions of certain countermeasures for use by children and offered potential solutions for state and local governments to consider when addressing this shortage. These solutions included assigning someone the responsibility of mixing suspensions at a POD site or compounding tablets of medical countermeasures into oral suspensions.[49]

In addition, CDC and FDA developed other guidance on dispensing medical countermeasures, including to the pediatric population, which could be shared with and used by state and local governments. For example, CDC developed a website and training opportunities for state and local governments to use when planning for dispensing medical countermeasures. The information shared through the website and training addresses dispensing in general, for the most part, although a small portion of the training touches on dispensing to the pediatric population. FDA also developed guidance on dispensing pediatric medical countermeasures. For example, because it can be difficult for children to swallow pills, FDA developed instructions for how to crush and mix doxycycline with water and then add to food to mask the taste of doxycycline. Additionally, FDA, with CDC, developed an information sheet about using doxycycline for the prevention of anthrax that state and local governments could share with their populations during an event. This sheet included dosing instructions for administering doxycycline to children.

CDC and FDA also collaborated to prepare, in advance of an actual CBRN incident, information about medical countermeasures that require an EUA or IND to have ready to share with state and local governments should an emergency occur.[50] This included information about how a countermeasure would be dispensed to children under an EUA or IND protocol, should there be a need. State and local governments could

---

[49]CDC has developed a new version of this guidance, which CDC has tentatively scheduled for release during calendar year 2013.

[50]This information is not shared with state and local governments in advance of a CBRN incident because medical countermeasures that are dispensed under an EUA or IND protocol have not been FDA-approved for use for these indications, according to HHS officials. Information about using medical countermeasures for these indications can change as new data are made available, and FDA and CDC wait to release such information until an emergency occurs to ensure that the information reflects the most recent data available.

then, in turn, share this information with their populations in the event of an emergency. For example, CDC and FDA developed an EUA fact sheet with instructions for administering doxycycline to children at home. CDC officials told us that they have information available for all medical countermeasures that could be used by children under an EUA. Information about pediatric dispensing under an EUA or IND protocol would be sent electronically—rather than in hard copy—to state and local governments because dispensing information can change and hard copies could become outdated.

State and Local Government Plans Provide Details about Pediatric Dispensing

State and local governments have provided details about pediatric dispensing in their emergency response plans. All seven of the state response plans we reviewed addressed the dispensing of countermeasures to the pediatric population during a CBRN incident.[51] Although the states' plans varied in format, they were consistent with one another in terms of the type of information they included about dispensing to children. For example, more than half of the states included information about pediatric dosing or formulations. Additionally, all seven states adopted some version of a "family member pick-up" policy—sometimes referred to as a "head of household" policy—which would allow adults to pick up medicines for other family members, including children, during an event. This policy is intended to eliminate disruptions to the dispensing process while simultaneously reducing patient numbers and increasing the number of persons treated during an incident. In addition, each state's plan provided other information about how medical countermeasures would be dispensed to children, either under a family member pick-up policy or through a POD.[52] For example,

- One state's medical countermeasure dispensing guidance noted that a POD should have specialized items for dispensing to children, such as scales for weighing children (if they are present and their parents do not know their weights) and mixing equipment to make pediatric portions. Additionally, the state's Point of Dispensing Field Operations

---

[51]Officials from one additional state also provided us with written information about its plans, but did not provide us with supporting documents to review.

[52]Despite having a family member pick-up policy in place, there are still reasons why a child might go to a POD. For example, parents might not want to be separated from their children during a CBRN incident, or unaccompanied minors may go to the POD looking for medication.

Guide suggested that the POD include a staff member who can be responsible for ensuring drugs are properly packaged and instructions for children are given.

- One state's plan discussed how oral antibiotic suspensions and syrups would be provided for the treatment of children who have trouble swallowing tablets, and that converting ciprofloxacin and doxycycline tablets into oral suspensions was recommended as an alternative for providing additional quantities of pediatric prophylactic regimens, due to the limited quantities of oral suspensions in the SNS. The plan included instructions for reconstituting these medical countermeasures.

- One state's plan provided information about dispensing countermeasures to unaccompanied children who request treatment at PODs. The issue of consent for emergency care to a child in a disaster was discussed.[53] Officials from this state told us that it works closely with the state's health care coalitions to ensure that the regional guidelines include pediatric-focused strategies.[54] Additionally, because pediatric doses are not stored in the SNS in large quantities, the state and local jurisdictions rely on partnerships with community and chain pharmacies to compound and reconstitute medications for children in an emergency.

As we found with the states, all seven of the local governments that provided us with plans addressed dispensing countermeasures for the pediatric population during a CBRN incident.[55] Like the states' plans, the local governments' plans varied in their format but were consistent with one another in terms of the type of information they included about dispensing to children. For example, more than half of the plans included information about screening children at a POD. Additionally, all seven local governments plan to implement versions of family member pick-up policies in the event of an emergency. The local governments' plans also

---

[53]In general, parental consent is required for the medical treatment of children.

[54]These health care coalitions, which support the state's health care preparedness program, work with local partners from different regions of the state to prepare hospitals, emergency medical service, and supporting health care organizations to deliver coordinated and effective care to individuals affected by public health emergencies.

[55]An official from one additional local government also spoke with us about its emergency response plans, but could not provide us with supporting documents to review.

included other ways to address the needs of the pediatric population when dispensing medical countermeasures. For example,

- One local government's POD plan described different types of dispensing, one of which is called "slow dispensing." Slow dispensing requires children under the age of 9 to pass through medical screenings, if they go to the POD.

- Another local government's plan described the setup of a special assistance station at a POD, where individuals could obtain medication for children under 9 years of age. Special assistance personnel could determine appropriate pediatric dosing by referring to available weight charts.

- Finally, one local government's plan discussed allowing "fast-tracking protocols," which would allow individuals with children to be diverted from the main lines and directed to a Help Desk to receive assistance.

CDC officials noted that state and local governments handle the dispensing of countermeasures to children in the same way as for adults; that is, the dispensing of countermeasures for both children and adults occurs at POD sites. However, CDC officials also told us that special considerations can still be made for children—for example, by establishing separate family lines in the PODs. We found examples of this consideration in some of the plans we reviewed.

Agency Comments

We provided a draft of this report to HHS for comment. In its written comments, reproduced in appendix II, HHS concurred with our findings. HHS reiterated information provided in our report, including that the development, procurement, and dispensing of medical countermeasures for the pediatric population is integrated into the PHEMCE's framework for public health preparedness across multiple component agencies, that state and local jurisdictions play an important role in responding to public health emergencies, and that the pace of progress in drug development is limited by the complex issues that surround the testing of countermeasures in children. In addition, HHS emphasized that the needs of the pediatric population have been a priority for HHS since the origins of Project Bioshield, and that the department is continuously progressing in this area. HHS also provided technical comments that we incorporated as appropriate.

We will send copies of this report to the Secretary of Health and Human Services and interested congressional committees. We will also make copies available at no charge on GAO's website at http://www.gao.gov.

If you or your staff have any questions about this report, please contact me at (202) 512-7114 or crossem@gao.gov. Contact points for our Offices of Congressional Relations and Public Affairs may be found on the last page of this report. Key contributors to this report are listed in appendix III.

Marcia Crosse
Director, Health Care

Appendix I: Pediatric CBRN Medical Countermeasures in the Strategic National Stockpile

Table 1 presents additional information about certain types of chemical, biological, radiological, and nuclear (CBRN) medical countermeasures available in the Strategic National Stockpile (SNS) by CBRN threat, as well as their regulatory status, for the pediatric population. The information presented is a general overview of countermeasures that are available for the pediatric population in the event of a CBRN incident, and does not include a complete list of all of the variations of each countermeasure.

Table 1: Overview of Certain Types of Chemical, Biological, Radiological, and Nuclear (CBRN) Medical Countermeasures Available in the Strategic National Stockpile (SNS) and Their Regulatory Status for the Pediatric Population

CBRN threat	Types of medical countermeasures available in the SNS	Regulatory status for the pediatric population[a]
Anthrax (*Bacillus anthracis*)	Oral solid antimicrobials	Three oral solid antimicrobials are available in the SNS to prevent or treat anthrax. One is approved for postexposure prophylaxis and treatment of anthrax in all children. Another is approved for postexposure prophylaxis for all children, but it is not approved for treatment of anthrax in any population. The third is not approved for postexposure prophylaxis or treatment of anthrax in any population. The antimicrobials that are not approved for postexposure prophylaxis or treatment would need to be used under an Emergency Use Authorization (EUA) for unapproved age groups, including adults, for these indications.
	Oral liquid antimicrobials	Three oral liquid antimicrobials are available in the SNS to prevent or treat anthrax. One is approved for postexposure prophylaxis and treatment of anthrax in all children. Another is approved for postexposure prophylaxis for all children, but it is not approved for treatment of anthrax in any population. The third is not approved for postexposure prophylaxis or treatment of anthrax in any population. The antimicrobials that are not approved for postexposure prophylaxis or treatment would need to be used under an EUA for unapproved age groups, including adults, for these indications.
	IV antimicrobials	Seven IV antimicrobials are available in the SNS to treat anthrax. Two have been approved for use by all children for the treatment of anthrax, and five have not been approved for the treatment of anthrax in any population. The antimicrobials that are not approved for the treatment of anthrax would need to be used under an EUA for all populations for this indication.
	Vaccine	One anthrax vaccine is available in the SNS, but it has not been approved for administration to children. It would need to be administered under an Investigational New Drug (IND) protocol.
	Antitoxin or immunoglobulin[b]	Two antitoxins/immunoglobulins are available in the SNS for the treatment of anthrax. One is approved for use by children to treat anthrax, while the other is not. The unapproved product would need to be used under an EUA in both adults and children.

CBRN threat	Types of medical countermeasures available in the SNS	Regulatory status for the pediatric population[a]
Plague (*Yersinia pestis*)	Oral solid antimicrobials	Two oral solid antimicrobials are available in the SNS for postexposure prophylaxis of plague. One is approved for use by some children, while the other is not approved for postexposure prophylaxis of plague in any population. The first antimicrobial would need to be used under an EUA for use by unapproved age groups for postexposure prophylaxis of plague, and the second antimicrobial would need to be used under an EUA for this indication for all populations.
	Oral liquid antimicrobials	Two oral liquid antimicrobials are available in the SNS for postexposure prophylaxis of plague. One is approved for use by some children, while the other is not approved for postexposure prophylaxis of plague in any population. The first antimicrobial would need to be used under an EUA for use by unapproved age groups for postexposure prophylaxis of plague, and the second antimicrobial would need to be used under an EUA for this indication for all populations.
	IV antimicrobials	Four IV antimicrobials are available in the SNS to treat plague. Two are approved for use by some children, and two are not approved for the treatment of plague in any population. The antimicrobials that are not approved for all children would need to be used under EUA for unapproved age groups for this indication, and the antimicrobials that are not approved for the treatment of plague would need to be used under an EUA for all populations.
Tularemia (*Francisella tularensis*)	Oral solid antimicrobials	Two oral solid antimicrobials are available in the SNS for postexposure prophylaxis of tularemia. One is approved for use by some children for this indication, while the other is not approved for postexposure prophylaxis of tularemia in any age population. The first antimicrobial would need to be used under an EUA for use by unapproved age groups for postexposure prophylaxis of tularemia, and the second antimicrobial would need to be used under an EUA for this indication for all populations.
	Oral liquid antimicrobials	Two oral liquid antimicrobials are available in the SNS for postexposure prophylaxis of tularemia. One is approved for use by some children for this indication, while the other is not approved for postexposure prophylaxis of tularemia in any age population. The first antimicrobial would need to be used under an EUA for use by unapproved age groups for postexposure prophylaxis of tularemia, and the second antimicrobial would need to be used under an EUA for this indication for all populations.
	IV antimicrobials	Four IV antimicrobials are available in the SNS to treat tularemia. One is approved for use by some children for the treatment of tularemia, and the other three are not approved for this indication in any age populations. The antimicrobial that is approved for use in some children for the treatment of tularemia would need to be used under an EUA by unapproved age groups. The other three antimicrobials that are not approved would need to be used under an EUA for this indication for all populations.

CBRN threat	Types of medical countermeasures available in the SNS	Regulatory status for the pediatric population[a]
Typhus (*Rickettsia prowazekii*)	Oral solid antimicrobials	One oral solid antimicrobial is available in the SNS to treat typhus, and it is approved for use by some children for this indication. This antimicrobial would need to be used under an EUA to treat typhus in unapproved populations.
	Oral liquid antimicrobials	One oral liquid antimicrobial is available in the SNS to treat typhus, and it is approved for use by some children for this indication. This antimicrobial would need to be used under an EUA to treat typhus in unapproved populations.
	IV antimicrobials	One IV antimicrobial is available in the SNS to treat typhus, and it is approved for use by some children for this indication. This antimicrobial would need to be used under an EUA to treat typhus in unapproved populations.
Botulism (Botulinum toxins)	Antitoxin or immunoglobulin	Two antitoxins are available in the SNS to treat botulism, and one is approved. The unapproved antitoxin would need to be used under an EUA to treat botulism. The approved product can be used in all populations, including children, under its license.
Smallpox (Variola virus)	Vaccine	Three smallpox vaccines are available in the SNS. One vaccine is approved for use by all children, and the other two are not approved for any age populations. These vaccines would need to be used under an EUA or an IND protocol.
	Antitoxin or immunoglobulin[b]	One immunoglobulin is available in the SNS for treatment of adverse reactions to the smallpox vaccine, and it is approved for use by all populations.
	IV antivirals	One IV antiviral is available in the SNS to treat adverse reactions to the smallpox vaccine, but it has not been approved for this indication for any age population. This antiviral would need to be used under an IND protocol for this indication.
Radiation (Radiological/nuclear agents)	Oral chelator[c]	One oral chelator is available in the SNS for treatment of internal radiation contamination, and it is approved for use by some children. This product would need to be used under an EUA for unapproved age groups for this indication.
	IV chelator[c]	Two IV chelators are available in the SNS for treatment of internal radiation contamination, and both have been approved for use by all children.
	Hematopoietic growth factors[d]	One hematopoietic growth factor is available in the SNS, but it has not been approved for use by any age population for the treatment of acute radiation syndrome. This product would need to be used under an EUA or an IND protocol for this indication.
Chemical (Nerve agents)	Nerve agent antidotes	Three nerve agent antidotes are available in the SNS for the treatment of poisoning by chemical nerve agents. Two of the antidotes have been approved for use by all children for this indication. The third antidote has an approved indication for use in seizures, but it has not been approved for use by all children and would need to be used under an EUA or an IND protocol for unapproved age groups.

Source: GAO summary of Centers for Disease Control and Prevention (CDC) and Food and Drug Administration (FDA) information.

Notes: According to CDC officials, in general, the same medical countermeasures are used for adults and children. The difference may be in weight-based dosing, or the need to use the medical countermeasures under a regulatory mechanism such as an EUA or IND. CDC officials stated that *Burkholderia mallei* (glanders), *Burkholderia pseudomallei* (melioidosis), and multi-drug resistant *Bacillus anthracis* are currently undergoing discussion for further planning. There are no medical countermeasures available for viral hemorrhagic fevers—Ebola, Marburg, and Junin viruses. In addition to the CBRN medical countermeasures listed, CDC officials told us that the SNS contains ventilators in pediatric sizes for all age groups down to 5 kilograms, as well as thermal burn supplies such as bandages, burn creams, and anti-nausea medications.

[a]FDA determined whether an EUA or IND protocol would be needed; we did not evaluate these determinations.

[b]Immunoglobulins are derived from blood plasma obtained from donors who have been immunized with a vaccine, and they contain ant bodies specific to the disease they are being used to treat.

[c]Chelators help remove certain radioactive particles from the body.

[d]Following radiation exposure, bone marrow can be suppressed. This reduces circulating white blood cells and increases the chance of infection. Infection can be prevented or mitigated by certain hematopoietic growth factors that activate bone marrow to protect from infection.

Appendix II: Comments from the Department of Health and Human Services

DEPARTMENT OF HEALTH & HUMAN SERVICES

OFFICE OF THE SECRETARY

Assistant Secretary for Legislation
Washington, DC 20201

APR 08 2013

Marcia Crosse
Director, Health Care
U.S. Government Accountability Office
441 G Street NW
Washington, DC 20548

Dear Ms. Crosse:

Attached are comments on the U.S. Government Accountability Office's (GAO) report entitled, "NATIONAL PREPAREDNESS: Efforts to Address the Medical Needs of Children in a Chemical, Biological, Radiological, or Nuclear Incident" (GAO 13-438).

The Department appreciates the opportunity to review this report prior to publication.

Sincerely,

Jim R. Esquea
Assistant Secretary for Legislation

Attachment

**GENERAL COMMENTS OF THE DEPARTMENT OF HEALTH AND HUMAN
SERVICES (HHS) ON THE GOVERNMENT ACCOUNTABILITY OFFICE'S (GAO)
DRAFT REPORT ENTITLED, "NATIONAL PREPAREDNESS: EFFORTS TO
ADDRESS THE MEDICAL NEEDS OF CHILDREN IN A CHEMICAL, BIOLOGICAL,
RADIOLOGICAL, OR NUCLEAR INCIDENT" (GAO-13-438)**

The Department appreciates the opportunity to review and comment on this draft report.

HHS greatly values the time and attention that GAO has devoted to this important topic and
overall we believe that the report does an admirable job of compiling a significant amount of
information on a sensitive and complex subject in addressing the needs of one of the most
vulnerable sectors of our population, our children.

The development, procurement, and dispensing of medical countermeasures for the pediatric
population (and other at-risk groups) is integrated into the general framework for public health
preparedness across the component agencies of the Public Health Emergency Medical
Countermeasures Enterprise (PHEMCE), which include the Office of the Assistant Secretary for
Preparedness and Response (ASPR), the Food and Drug Administration, the National Institutes
of Health (NIH), and the Centers for Disease Control and Prevention. The PHEMCE recognizes
the unique challenges resulting from both the regulatory and product formulation issues
associated with pediatric needs, and has chosen very deliberately to enhance our efforts to
address these concerns.

In 2012, PHEMCE released a new *Strategy* and *Implementation Plan*, which establish meeting
the needs of at-risk populations as a central goal of the Enterprise. Specifically, the documents
call for increasing our focus on at-risk populations in medical consequence and public health
response assessments and requirements setting, supporting medical countermeasures
development for at-risk populations, and ensuring coordinated and equitable access to medical
countermeasures across all populations.

One of PHEMCE's key responsibilities is overseeing the requirements-setting process for
medical countermeasures. Our Integrated Product Teams (IPTs) are working groups tasked with
identifying and prioritizing gaps in our capabilities. To ensure that cross-cutting pediatric (and
obstetric) population issues are addressed, the PHEMCE established the Obstetrics and Pediatrics
IPT. IPT membership is drawn from subject matter experts across the component agencies,
representing a collaborative approach to address pediatric needs, as well as those of other at-risk
groups.

Finally, the PHEMCE, through the auspices of the ASPR's role in formulating issues for the
National Biodefense Science Board (NBSB), has recently opined on the difficult question of how
best to approach the gathering of safety data for biodefense products that do not have specific
indication for pediatric populations. After careful thought, the NBSB concluded that, weighing
the risks to the patient, as well as theoretical impacts on post-event operational issues for product
use, the gathering of safety data prior to an event was preferable to doing so after an event. This
issue was then given national attention when considered by the President's Commission on
Bioethics for further debate and resolution, as discussed in the Commission's recently released
report.

1

GENERAL COMMENTS OF THE DEPARTMENT OF HEALTH AND HUMAN SERVICES (HHS) ON THE GOVERNMENT ACCOUNTABILITY OFFICE'S (GAO) DRAFT REPORT ENTITLED, "NATIONAL PREPAREDNESS: EFFORTS TO ADDRESS THE MEDICAL NEEDS OF CHILDREN IN A CHEMICAL, BIOLOGICAL, RADIOLOGICAL, OR NUCLEAR INCIDENT" (GAO-13-438)

In 2010, ASPR established the Children's HHS Interagency Leadership on Disasters (CHILD) Working Group to identify and comprehensively integrate the activities related to the needs of children across all HHS inter- and intra-governmental disaster planning activities and operations. The CHILD Working Group developed six recommendations specific to pediatric medical countermeasures, as described in its 2011 report.

On the operational side, ASPR is engaged in a number of activities that address the unique needs of children during a disaster. The Hospital Preparedness Program grants and cooperative agreements include guidance to states to assure that written plans and exercises include provisions for at-risk populations, including pediatric patients. The National Disaster Medical System (NDMS) is directed by a pediatrician with advanced fellowship training in pre-hospital and disaster medicine. This ensures that NDMS has ongoing perspectives to the specific vulnerabilities of children in disaster, and positions NDMS well to develop programs to meet these needs. Finally, ASPR has developed playbooks for each of the National Planning Scenarios. Each of these playbooks specifically integrates operational considerations, resources, and action items targeting requirements for pediatric and other at-risk populations.

We would like to emphasize that the unique and complex needs of the pediatric population have been a priority for HHS since at least the origins of Project Bioshield. This commitment was solidified with the passage of the Pandemic and All-Hazards Preparedness Act in 2006 and re-affirmed in its recent reauthorization. There has been an enduring commitment and products that have been procured to protect this population segment, or are in development now, have long been part of the national preparedness agenda.

We would also like to reiterate that the pace of substantial progress in drug development and approval for the pediatric population is not a matter of HHS policy. Progress is largely limited by the complex issues that surround the testing of countermeasures in children. This was recently directly demonstrated by the recommendations from the President's Commission on Bioethics, which once again re-affirmed the very limited allowance given on regulatory issues related to developing products for pediatric populations. These ethical issues, bound by regulatory language regarding direct benefit for pediatric populations in clinical trials, are not directed specifically at products associated with the types of public health emergency situations confronted by the PHEMCE, but do directly affect its ability to easily achieve the desired results. As one example of clinical trial progress in medical countermeasures applied to pediatric populations, as well as adult populations, the NIH-funded RAMPART study was recently recognized as the top clinical trial of 2012. This trial evaluated midazolam as an effective treatment for seizure activity in epilepsy and is directly relevant to the ability to treat pediatric patients with this drug following a nerve agent exposure.

In addition, from an operational perspective, it is important to recognize the important role that our non-federal partners play in responding to emergencies and disasters, including CBRN incidents. The federal government is not the sole or major provider for such responses. The capabilities and resiliency of state and local jurisdictions cannot be underestimated. Particularly

2

**GENERAL COMMENTS OF THE DEPARTMENT OF HEALTH AND HUMAN
SERVICES (HHS) ON THE GOVERNMENT ACCOUNTABILITY OFFICE'S (GAO)
DRAFT REPORT ENTITLED, "NATIONAL PREPAREDNESS: EFFORTS TO
ADDRESS THE MEDICAL NEEDS OF CHILDREN IN A CHEMICAL, BIOLOGICAL,
RADIOLOGICAL, OR NUCLEAR INCIDENT" (GAO-13-438)**

for small chemical, biological, radiological, and nuclear incidents, the scale and timing of the
incident have not historically required federal intervention beyond providing expertise and
supporting coordination. While there are some countermeasures that only exist in federal caches,
the actual use of them relies on local capability and fairly robust distribution networks exist.

We thank you once again for your breadth of coverage on these important issues, for your overall
assessment that HHS and the PHEMCE has devoted considerable attention to this need, and for
acknowledging that we are continuously progressing in tackling this complex work.

3

Appendix III: GAO Contact and Staff Acknowledgments

GAO Contact	Marcia Crosse, (202) 512-7114 or crossem@gao.gov
Staff Acknowledgments	In addition to the contact named above, Tom Conahan, Assistant Director; Kaitlin Coffey; Kelly DeMots; Carolina Morgan; Monica Perez-Nelson; and Roseanne Price made key contributions to this report.

Related GAO Products

National Preparedness: Improvements Needed for Measuring Awardee Performance in Meeting Medical and Public Health Preparedness Goals. GAO-13-278. Washington, D.C.: March 22, 2013.

National Preparedness: Countermeasures for Thermal Burns. GAO-12-304R. Washington, D.C.: February 22, 2012.

Chemical, Biological, Radiological, and Nuclear Risk Assessments: DHS Should Establish More Specific Guidance for Their Use. GAO-12-272. Washington, D.C.: January 25, 2012.

National Preparedness: Improvements Needed for Acquiring Medical Countermeasures to Threats from Terrorism and Other Sources. GAO-12-121. Washington, D.C.: October 26, 2011.

National Preparedness: DHS and HHS Can Further Strengthen Coordination for Chemical, Biological, Radiological, and Nuclear Risk Assessments. GAO-11-606. Washington, D.C.: June 21, 2011.

Public Health Preparedness: Developing and Acquiring Medical Countermeasures Against Chemical, Biological, Radiological, and Nuclear Agents. GAO-11-567T. Washington, D.C.: April 13, 2011.

National Security: Key Challenges and Solutions to Strengthen Interagency Collaboration. GAO-10-822T. Washington, D.C.: June 9, 2010.

Combating Nuclear Terrorism: Actions Needed to Better Prepare to Recover from Possible Attacks Using Radiological or Nuclear Materials. GAO-10-204. Washington, D.C.: January 29, 2010.

Project BioShield Act: HHS Has Supported Development, Procurement, and Emergency Use of Medical Countermeasures to Address Health Threats. GAO-09-878R. Washington, D.C.: July 24, 2009.

Project BioShield: HHS Can Improve Agency Internal Controls for Its New Contracting Authorities. GAO-09-820. Washington, D.C.: July 21, 2009.

Project BioShield: Actions Needed to Avoid Repeating Past Problems with Procuring New Anthrax Vaccine and Managing the Stockpile of Licensed Vaccine. GAO-08-88. Washington, D.C.: October 23, 2007.

www.ingramcontent.com/pod-product-compliance
Lightning Source LLC
Chambersburg PA
CBHW080627290526
45790CB00007B/2956